Great Moments in SPORTS

by RITA GOLDEN GELMAN

SCHOLASTIC BOOK SERVICES

NEW YORK · TORONTO · LONDON · AUCKLAND · SYDNEY · TOKYO

With special thanks
to Mitch Gelman
for his assistance

Cover photos: Focus on Sports

Photo Credits

Wide World Photos: pp. 8-9, p. 37, p. 40, p. 43, p. 49, pp. 56-58, pp. 67-69, p. 73, pp. 77-800, pp. 87-88, pp. 95-96, p. 105, pp. 111-112, pp. 123-124; Malcolm W. Emmons/NFL Properties, Inc.: p. 10; Fred Roe/NFL Properties, Inc.: p. 13; NFL Properties, Inc.: p. 14; Raphael/NFL Properties, Inc.: p. 16; UPI: pp. 21-22, pp. 26-27, p. 32, p. 36, p. 41 p. 50, p. 62, p. 74, p. 114, p. 119, p. 127.

ISBN 0-590-31311-8

Copyright © 1980 by Rita Golden Gelman. All rights reserved. Published by Scholastic Book Services, a Division of Scholastic Magazines, Inc.

12 11 10 9 8 7 6 5 4 3 2 1   9   0 1 2 3 4 5/8

Printed in the U.S.A.   21

Contents

To the reader

There are many different *kinds* of great moments in sports.

Some moments are great and memorable because of the excitement they create: an unexpected catch to win a game; an underdog team that runs all over the favorite; a ballgame that changes its lead every few minutes.

There are other memorable moments, as when a person achieves true perfection in his or her performance of a sport. Or when a great and experienced athlete, who has had many triumphs, attains a special goal — the peak of a lifetime of hard work and achievement. And finally, there are those tender moments when a sports crowd demonstrates its love and respect for a great human being, paying homage to that athlete for his or her contributions to the world.

Your favorite sports event or hero may not be here. You may not agree with all the choices. But the book has succeeded if, after reading it, you find you have enjoyed sharing the great events and meeting the athletes who made those events happen.

Football

THE FRANCO HARRIS CATCH

**Pittsburgh Steelers vs. Oakland Raiders
December 23, 1972**

Somehow, out of nowhere, it came. A gift from the sky. Franco Harris had caught hundreds of passes before. And he would go on to catch many more. But when people speak about "The Franco Harris Catch," they are speaking about the one he caught on December 23, 1972, in the first round of the National Football League playoffs.

It was a cold day at Three Rivers Stadium in Pittsburgh, but tension was high. By the third quarter, the Oakland Raiders and the Pittsburgh Steelers were still locked in a 0 − 0 defensive battle.

Daryle Lamonica, then the Raiders' quarterback, couldn't get his team into Pittsburgh territory. Five times he drove to the middle of the field. And five times he was stopped.

Pittsburgh wasn't exactly racking up the touchdowns either. By the beginning of the fourth quarter, the score was only 6 – 0, Pittsburgh. The points had come from two field goals.

Oakland took out Lamonica and put in a substitute quarterback, a very young Ken Stabler. With four minutes left, the Raiders finally crossed the midfield line to Pittsburgh's 30.

On the next play, Pittsburgh tried to blitz. Stabler slipped back, ran around the blitz, and raced 30 yards, untouched, to tie up the game. And a Senior Raider, George Blanda — with a little over one minute left to the game — kicked for the point. The score was 7 – 6, Oakland Raiders.

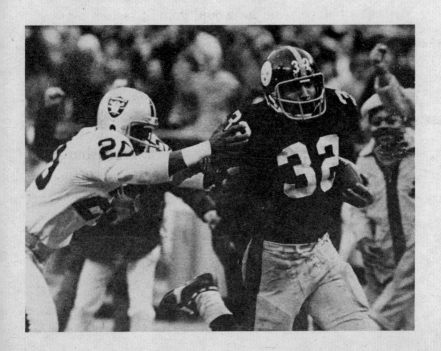

It looked like the end for Pittsburgh, as the clock ticked away the seconds. 10, 9, 8, 7, 6.... Only a miracle could save them. Then, it happened!

With only five seconds left, Steeler quarterback Terry Bradshaw went back to throw a desperation pass to receiver John (Frenchy) Fuqua. Raider Jack Tatum saw the ball coming. Tatum raced toward Fuqua and the airborne football. The two men collided, and the speeding ball hit the combined mass of Tatum and Fuqua and bounced into the air.

That was it. The game was over. But it wasn't! Suddenly, out of nowhere, Pittsburgh's Franco Harris was there. He grabbed the ball out of the air and kept running. Right into the end zone.

People shook their heads. A second earlier there had been no one around. Harris really had come out of nowhere. Harris had been in the backfield blocking, heading downfield, when he saw Bradshaw throw the pass. "I thought I might get there in time to block for him," said Harris, later. "Just as I put it in gear, I saw the ball bounce into the air. I said to myself, 'Oh, no. It's all over.' Then I saw that it was bouncing toward me, and I felt I might get it if I kept going. I did."

Harris made the catch seven yards back from the collision. He ran 42 yards for the touchdown. 13 – 7, Pittsburgh. The game was over. But the controversy wasn't. There was a rule in pro football then that a pass could not be touched by two offensive players, one after the other, unless a defensive player also touched it. That meant that if the pass had bounced off Fuqua, into Harris' arms, it was no good. It had to have been touched by Tatum.

"I never did hit the ball," said Tatum. "No comment," said Fuqua.

The referees huddled briefly just after the play. They even consulted with NFL officials who were in the press box studying the instant replay. They all agreed. It was a touchdown. Pittsburgh had won the game.

And so went one of the freakiest — and most famous — plays in football history.

JOE NAMATH'S GREATEST DAY

Super Bowl: New York Jets vs. Baltimore Colts
January 12, 1969

It was a big joke. A Super Bowl between the unbeatable Baltimore Colts of the National Football League and the nowhere New York Jets of the American Football League. It would be a blood-bath, not a football game, predicted the experts. Baltimore was clearly the better team.

The Colts had won thirteen of their season's four-teen games. Their defense had blitzed through of-fenses all season. They had buried quarterbacks and bulldozed the biggest and best opponents. It was practically impossible to score against them. In the last ten games, the Colts had given up only seven touchdowns.

As for the Jets, it was true they had come a long way from the days when they could barely win a game. Their star quarterback, Joe Namath, had given them an exciting season. He was thrilling to watch in action, and most everyone agreed that Namath was a great passer. The Jets had lost only three games, playing against American Football League teams. But they had never come up against competition like the Baltimore Colts.

At that time, the American Football League was in its early years. Other AFL champion teams had been mauled in the first two Super Bowls. So it didn't mean much to the experts that the Jets were AFL champions. According to people who knew, the Jets didn't belong on the same field as the Baltimore Colts. The game was going to be a slaughter. Everyone knew that.

But someone forgot to tell Joe Namath.

Joe marched into Miami as though he and his Jets were superheroes. "We're going to win on Sunday. I

guarantee it!" he announced to the world. "We're number one." The experts laughed and made the Jets eighteen-point underdogs.

But Joe wasn't listening to the experts. He had made an interesting discovery. He had studied movies of the Colts. He had especially studied the famous Baltimore blitz. In his autobiography, *I Can't Wait Until Tomorrow*, Joe wrote what he had discovered:

> Sometimes, one safety would blitz — shoot through and try to get the quarterback — and, sometimes, the other would blitz. No matter who blitzed, they had to leave part of the middle open. I knew I could hit my wide receivers slanting in.

Joe was excited. So were his teammates. Later, he wrote, "I wondered which one of us was going to call up the Colts and tell them they didn't have a chance." But no one had to call the Colts. Joe ran around Miami telling everyone, "We're going to win. There's no doubt about it."

By the time the fans poured into Miami's Orange Bowl, there was a rumble of doubt in the stands. Could the experts have been wrong? Was Namath just being brash? Or was there really a chance that the Jets could win?

The first quarter of the game gave only a hint that the experts might have been wrong. The Colts looked good as they moved down the field — but

they couldn't get the ball in the end zone, except for one failed field goal attempt.

In the next quarter, the Colts succeeded in getting the ball into the end zone with a pass from the Colt quarterback, Earl Morall — but it dropped into the hands of a Jet defender.

Then the game seemed to turn. Namath called running plays. The Jets moved down the field. He called pass plays. They kept moving. They moved all the way to the first touchdown of the game. The Jets, not the Colts, were controlling the ball, and Namath's plays were thrilling to watch.

Early in the fourth quarter, the Jets made it 10 – 0 on a field goal from the 25-yard line. Two more field goals made the score 16 – 0.

In the last three minutes of the game, Baltimore's veteran Johnny Unitas, who had replaced Earl Morall, managed to get the Colts a touchdown. But the final score was 16 – 7, Jets.

Joe Namath had led the underdog New York Jets to a Super Bowl victory, the first Super Bowl to be won by an AFL team! Namath leaped into the air, pointing toward the sky. "Number one," he was saying. "The Jets are the best."

And the experts, choking on their predictions, had to agree.

O.J. PASSES 2,000

Buffalo Bills vs. New York Jets
December 17, 1973

O.J. Simpson, tough kid and local gang leader,
recognized Jim Brown immediately. O.J. had just
seen the great running back for the Cleveland
Browns on the football field. Now they were both
standing in the same ice cream store. And so were a
bunch of O.J.'s friends.

O.J. decided to put on a big-man act for his
friends. He walked over to Brown. "Listen, man,"
said O.J. to Brown. "I'm gonna break *all* your
records." Brown couldn't believe it. He just stared
at the kid. Then he said, "Let's see what you do
when you get the chance."

Years later, when O.J. was no longer a kid and no
longer a gang leader, he was still tough—at least on
the football field. O.J. was a star running back for

the Buffalo Bills. And he was still after Jim Brown's records, especially the one for most yards in a single season—1,863. Brown had set the record in 1963. No one had come close to breaking it until 1973, the year of O.J. Simpson.

The year before, O.J. had led the NFL in yards rushed, 1,251. Before the 1973 season began, O.J. and some of his teammates were sitting around, talking. "Hey," said O.J. "This year we get 1,700." "If you're going for 1,700, why not 2,000? What's 300 yards?" said a friend. Everyone laughed. Two thousand yards was impossible. It couldn't be done.

But as the 1973 season rolled along, so did the Buffalo Bills. "Man," said one of the players. "When we're rolling, no one can stop us." And hardly anyone did. All season, O.J., The Juice, and his line, known as "The Electric Company" because they turned on The Juice, just kept rolling in those yards.

Time after time, tacklers would lunge at the twisting, turning number 32. And time after time they would end up on the ground alone while O.J. sprinted down the field. "O.J. senses tacklers," said one of his teammates. "He makes cuts that are uncanny. It's almost like the guy coming up behind him is yelling, 'Here I come. You better go the other way.' " Before the final game of the season, O.J. had run for 1,803 yards, 61 yards short of breaking the record.

"The night before the final game," his roommate said, "he was real uptight. I heard him tossing and turning all night."

Tense and wakeful, O.J. thought about the men who had blocked for him all season. The men of the Electric Company who had opened up holes for him to run through. The men who had made it possible for him to gain so many yards. "Open it up, open it up for The Juice," they had shouted to each other all season. O.J. knew he couldn't have done it alone.

He certainly wasn't alone the next day on the New York Jets' snowy Shea Stadium field. At 1:25, with four minutes and 26 seconds left in the first quarter, Buffalo's quarterback, Joe Ferguson, knelt in the huddle. "One-five right," he told the offensive line. Then he took the snap and handed the ball to O.J. Six yards later, O.J.'s dreams came true. The record collapsed. O.J.'s season total was 1,869, six yards better than the best ever.

The referee stopped the game. He handed O.J. the ball and shook his hand. O.J. trotted to the sidelines, his arms high. The fans cheered. But O.J.'s teammates still weren't satisfied. Oh, they slapped hands. They shouted a little. "Way to go, Juice." But they weren't finished. "More, Juice. More," they chanted. "Let's get more." And they went on with the game.

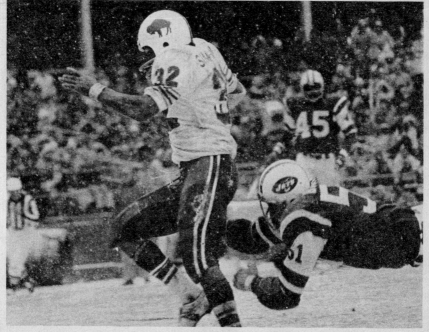

Three quarters later, with five minutes and 56 seconds left in the game, O.J. carried the ball for seven yards—and 2,003 for the season. There had never been a season like it. O.J. had done the undreamable. He had passed the 2,000 mark.

Now the Bills were ready to celebrate. The whole team raced onto the field. They hoisted O.J. onto their shoulders. O.J. raised his left fist in victory. The fans cheered. The team jumped around the field, screaming, slapping each other in joy.

At a special press conference after the game, reporters were eager to talk to O.J. They wanted to ask him how it felt to be the greatest. But O.J. walked into the interview with the whole offensive unit. "These," he said, "are the cats who did the job all year long." Then he introduced them all.

O.J. was the greatest, the best. O.J. had made football history. But he didn't forget the guys who had brought him to the top. He knew he couldn't have done it alone.

A GAME TO REMEMBER

Sugar Bowl: Notre Dame vs. Alabama
December 31, 1973

Let's pretend for a minute that you are an avid rooter for either Notre Dame or the University of Alabama, and that you have just sat through the 1973 Sugar Bowl in New Orleans.

The following facts are certain:

If you are a screamer, you have no voice left.

If you are a nail-biter, you have no nails left.

If you like to pound the person next to you, that person is no longer next to you — and may, in fact, no longer exist!

This contest between two of the toughest teams in college football was *that* exciting. Here is a score-box of touchdowns, showing the number of times the lead changed.

Notre Dame	6	6	14	14	21	21	24
Alabama	0	7	7	17	17	23	23

And that doesn't give a clue to the number of nail-biting, scream-producing, pound-your-neighbor moments in the game.

Even before the game, the excitement began. Both teams were undefeated. And both were chomping for the championship. Bear Bryant, the Alabama coach, was on his way to becoming the winningest coach in college football. Known throughout the football world as a drill-sergeant kind of coach, he was tough and demanding.

He was also wary. Before the championship game, Bryant hired guards for each floor of the motel where his players were staying. He wanted to know what his players were doing. And he wanted to be sure that no strangers would be walking around, picking up information about Alabama's game plans. No one was allowed past the guards without a pass signed by Bryant.

Ara Parsegian, the Notre Dame coach, was as concerned about security as Bryant. He wouldn't allow anyone to see Notre Dame's practices. Once, during a practice, Parsegian spotted a strange face in the press box. "A spy," he thought. And he immediately sent someone up to check out the stranger. The man was installing telephones.

Security was a major concern of both coaches. But there obviously was no security in the kitchen of the Alabama team's hotel. On the day of the game,

53 team breakfast steaks burned up in a kitchen fire. That didn't help the mood of the Alabama team.

And neither did the opening minutes of the game. Alabama discovered that Notre Dame had a whole new set of offensive and defensive plays. By the time Alabama was able to figure them out, the score was 6 – 0, Notre Dame. Screams. Cheers. Drums. From the Notre Dame side.

But Alabama wasn't down for long. The Alabama stands shook with screaming fans when Alabama took over the lead, 7 – 6.

But it was a short-lived lead. Notre Dame returned the kickoff for a 93-yard touchdown and another seven points. Cheerleaders cartwheeled. Trumpets blared. Fans shouted.

Notre Dame's halfback Al Hunter (25) racing 95 yards for a touchdown.

It wasn't a perfect game. But every minute was exciting. Even the mistakes. There were five fumbles in which the ball changed sides. Five screaming, pounding, fan-frenzied fumbles.

Alabama kept taking the lead, then losing it. When Notre Dame was ahead, 21 – 17, Bear Bryant called a surprise halfback to quarterback pass that made the score 23 – 21. The stadium shook with cheers and stamping feet.

Deep into the final quarter, with Alabama ahead, 23 – 21, Tom Clements, Notre Dame quarterback, began a drive. The team made its way down the

Notre Dame's quarterback Tom Clements (2) in action.

field, yard by yard. Three times Clements carried the ball himself. Then, he moved back to pass. Down the field, thirty yards away, Notre Dame's Dave Casper was boxed in by two Alabama players. Either one of them could have made an interception. But neither one did. Alabama's Ricky Davis thought that David McMakin was going to get it. But McMakin had lost the ball in the wind. Casper just reached out and caught the pass. The fans went wild. Notre Dame was in field goal position. The kick was good. 24 – 23, Notre Dame.

But even then the game wasn't over. With less than two minutes left to play, Notre Dame had the ball on its own two-yard line, third down. Every one of the battered fans knew what was going to happen. Clements was going to call a running play. It was the only thing to do. Notre Dame was in the lead and there were less than two minutes to play. A running play would help use up the time. A pass would have been crazy. There would have been too much danger of an interception or a safety. A running play was the only thing to do.

The play began. Clements took the ball from the center and handed off to the running back. No. Wait a second. He *faked* to the running back. Clements was in the end zone. He was going to pass! It was crazy. The stands were going mad. But not Clements. He calmly fired a 35-yard spiral to his lonely receiver. It was a first down. Alabama never saw the ball again.

A crazy, chaotic, wild finish to a crazy, chaotic, wild game. The fans exploded along with the final gun. They cheered as the battered, bruised, and ecstatically happy Notre Dame team left the field. They cheered as the battered, bruised, and disappointed Alabama team left the field. Even the cheering fans were battered and bruised. But all of them knew, as they finally walked through the gates, that they had been present for one of the most dramatic and suspenseful afternoons in sports.

Boxing

CHAMP FOR THE THIRD TIME

Heavyweight Championship Fight:
Muhammad Ali vs. Leon Spinks
September 15, 1978

The New Orleans airport had been a madhouse all afternoon. Now the New Orleans Superdome was swarming with 70,000 people. Together they had paid five million dollars to see the Muhammad Ali/ Leon Spinks heavyweight championship fight.

And millions of people were watching at home — sports fans, boxing fans, men, women, children. Even people who couldn't tell a boxing glove from a hamster were at their television sets. They were hoping to see Muhammad Ali become the first man in history to win the championship three times.

Once, in his own words, he had been "the boldest, the prettiest, the most skillfullest fighter ever." But that was a long time ago. Now Ali was thirty-six years old. Now, all those millions of people weren't even expecting to see skillful boxing. As one sportswriter put it, "Spinks hasn't yet learned how to fight. And Ali is no longer able."

No, they weren't there to see spectacular boxing. They were there because seven months earlier, a fat, sluggish, run-down Ali had lost his title to Spinks. And now, the man who had once been "The Greatest" was going into the ring for a last chance to go out as a champ. And millions of people were in his corner with him.

In his younger days, Ali had charmed the world. "I'm the fighter the world needs," he had said at the beginning of his career. "I have personality, color, patience, charm." And he was right. The dull sport of boxing sparkled while Ali was the champ.

He spouted verses. "Everyone knew when I stepped into town. I was the greatest fighter around," he said. He danced around the ring. He oozed with pride and confidence and humor. And he made everyone smile and feel a little more alive.

"I'm the prettiest fighter in the world," he said. "As pretty as a girl." And he stood on street corners and talked to kids — and made them happy. He joked with people on the streets — and made them laugh. He donated money to recreation centers, to needy people. He shared his fame. He shared his fortune. And he shared his bursting energy for life.

Ali talks with Leon Spinks.

An encounter with Muhammad Ali, even over television, made everyone feel a little bit more alive.

When he lost his title to Spinks, people said Ali was washed up. "The fire is out," said some. "He's over the hill." Ali was down. He wasn't spouting poetry. He wasn't jabbering. He wasn't laughing.

But Ali had been down before. He had been down when they took away his title in 1967 because he had refused to go into the Army. Like many other young people in the late 1960's, Ali had said that his beliefs prevented him from fighting in a war. He left it up to the courts to decide whether his refusal would be considered a crime.

But the boxing organization didn't wait for the courts. They didn't agree with Ali's beliefs, so they said he could no longer be the champion. They took away his title. And they told him he couldn't fight any more.

Ali's battle with the Army had nothing to do with boxing. But there he was at the top of his career — strong, confident, fast, young — and they told him he couldn't fight any more. For two-and-a-half years, while Ali's case was traveling through the courts, Ali was not allowed to fight. Not allowed to make a living the only way he knew.

Finally, in 1970, Ali was allowed to fight again. But the title was no longer his. And neither were the two-and-a-half years when his skills were at their very best. "It's too late," they were saying. "He's lost his best years."

But Ali was determined to win the title back. He fought Joe Frazier, the champ. He lost. Then he fought a whole string of other boxers, earning his right to get another crack at the champion.

By the time Ali fought Frazier again, Frazier was no longer the champion. Ali beat him and earned a chance to fight the new champion, George Foreman.

Foreman was considered a Superman. "No one can beat him," they said. "Foreman will be champion for ten years," they said. He was tough, he was powerful. He was the best.

The Ali/Foreman fight took place in Zaire, the

third largest nation in Africa. It was televised into thousands of theaters around the world.

"Ali, Ali, Ali, Ali," screamed the audience in Zaire. And when the fight was over, that's who it was. Ali was back where he belonged. People had said he was finished. But he was champ instead. The greatest, the prettiest, the boldest, the most talked about fighter in the world was back on the top. And everyone loved it.

In his prime, Ali was a boxer with extraordinary skill. He was fast. He danced around the ring in constant motion. When he was feeling super-confident, Ali would do a little hop-skip sort of dance step — the Ali shuffle. When he did the Ali shuffle, everyone knew that he was in control. That he was on top of the world. And millions of people would smile and feel a little more alive.

But in 1978, Ali wasn't in his prime any more. "Hang up the gloves," he was told when he lost his title to Spinks. "You've got the money. You've got the fame. Quit fighting."

But Ali never heard the words. His pride wouldn't let him. "The Greatest" wasn't going to quit without his title. So he booked a second fight with Spinks. And then he trained.

"Run," said his trainers. And Ali ran and ran and ran. "When I run," he said, "I want to stop, but I can't. My chest burns. My throat is dry. I feel like

I'm going to faint. My body begs me to stop. But I make myself run another mile, two more miles up those hills. Pain, all the time I'm in pain. I hurt all over. I hate it but I'm taking it. I'm making myself suffer. I have to suffer. I know this is my last fight and it's the last time I'll ever have to do it. Just a few more weeks of pain and suffering to live good all the rest of my life, to always be champion."

"Fight," said his trainer. And he fought. Round after round after round. Moving, jabbing, throwing a hook. Ali sparred more than two hundred rounds before the second Spinks fight. He had sparred less than twenty for the first one.

"Exercise," said his trainers. And every day Ali did hundreds of sit-ups, building his stomach muscles. "Never have I suffered like I'm forcing myself to suffer now. To win, all I need to do is suffer. I don't want to lose and then spend the rest of my life looking back and saying, 'I should have trained harder.' "

By September 15th, Ali was in terrific shape. On the night of the fight he looked ten years younger than he had in the first Spinks fight. And he had in his eyes a touch of that old pride and sparkle.

As everyone expected, it wasn't much of a fight — as far as boxing skills were concerned. Ali jabbed, jabbed, jabbed. Then he would throw a right. Then, as Spinks was coming at him, Ali would

grab Spinks around the back of his head and tie him up in a clinch. Then, when the referee broke it up, Ali would dance away, circle a few times, and do it all over again. Said one sportswriter, "Spinks spent the night throwing punches in places Ali had left several minutes before."

By the end of the seventh round, Ali knew he had won. When the bell rang, Ali did the Ali shuffle back to his corner. The Superdome went crazy. People screamed in front of their television sets. The old Ali was back. He was in control. He was doing his thing. It was like old times. Everyone smiled and felt a little more alive. It was a sloppy fight with all that grabbing and missing. "Sloppy?" said one of his trainers. "It was beautifully sloppy. It was gorgeous sloppy, wonderful sloppy."

The judges didn't comment on the sloppiness. They simply wrote on their cards: 10-4-1, 10-4-1,

11-4-0. Muhammad Ali was again the Heavyweight Champion of the world.

All around the world people cheered. Muhammad Ali had become the only fighter ever to win the title for the third time. He had won it for himself. He had won it for his fans. He had won it so that everyone in the world would feel just a little more alive.

Baseball

SANDY KOUFAX'S FOURTH NO-HITTER: A PERFECT GAME

Los Angeles Dodgers vs. Chicago Cubs
September 9, 1965

They fell like moving toy ducks at a carnival shooting gallery. One after another, the Chicago Cubs swung their way to the bench, overpowered by the fast balls and breaking pitches of lefty Dodger pitcher, Sandy Koufax.

It was Sandy's fourth no-hit, no-run game in four years. That's more no-hitters than any other pitcher in baseball history. But the game in Los Angeles was more than just a no-hitter. It was also a perfect game. Twenty-seven players in a row were wiped out. Not one Cub player made it to first base.

"I didn't have any particular stuff at the beginning of the game. Just average," Sandy wrote in his autobiography, *Koufax*. "I was throwing mostly curves through the early innings." And in those early innings, both Koufax and Bob Hendley, the Cub pitcher, had no-hitters going. Neither pitcher allowed a hit until, in the seventh inning, Dodger Lou Johnson hit a little blooper down the right field line. If it had been fielded well, it wouldn't have been a hit. But it wasn't Hendley's day for luck, and the little blooper became a hit. The only run of the game had come in the fifth inning when Johnson had walked, was sacrificed to second, stole third, and shot home on the catcher's wild throw.

Sandy still had his no-hitter going into the eighth inning. The score was 1 − 0, Dodgers. The Cubs had

no hits and no walks. But all it takes to stop the perfect game is one line drive to the right place. One blooper, poorly fielded. One walk.

The tension was tremendous coming into the eighth inning. Sandy faced Ron Santo and Ernie Banks, two of the Cubs' hardest hitting players. Sandy stayed cool. He just threw his pitches over the plate. "My fastball really came alive," said Sandy. "I was throwing as good a fastball as I had all year." Santo and Banks struck out. And so did a rookie left fielder.

Now there were only three outs to go. 29,139 fans held their breath as the first batter in the ninth inning struck out. They swallowed hard as the second batter went down. And they leaped from their seats screaming as the third player went down swinging. Sandy Koufax had his perfect game. Like every other pitcher in baseball, he had dreamed of that day.

Once, Sandy's dreams had been different. Once he had been a basketball player dreaming of the 100-point game. When Sandy was in high school in Brooklyn, New York, his passion was basketball. On one occasion he had a chance to play basketball against the New York Knicks. "That kid has amazing leaping ability and amazing strength," said one of the Knicks. "We'll be coming back for him some day."

But they never did. Sandy did have the leap. And he had tremendous shooting skill. But he also had a problem. He fired the passes so hard that no one could touch them. Sandy's throws usually shot past his teammates and bounced off the wall of the gym. "He fired too hard for a basketball player," said his high school coach.

But when Sandy tried pitching baseball a few years later, his stinging, fierce fastball was his finest weapon. The Dodgers signed him in 1954. At first, he barely knew anything about baseball. "All he had was speed," said Joe Becker, the Dodger pitching coach. "He couldn't do anything right. We had to take him behind the barracks and show him

how to stand on the mound, how to release the ball."

Becker also had to teach Sandy that throwing too hard could get him in trouble. "Trying to superspeed every time you're in a jam hurts you," Becker told Sandy. "Your muscles tighten and you can't throw properly. When a pitcher tenses up and tries to throw too hard, that's when he gets in trouble. When he relaxes and throws with a nice, loose wrist, his pitches do things."

By the time Sandy pitched his perfect game, he had learned how to relax. But he had another problem — a physical problem. His doctors told him he had arthritis in his elbow. They told him that if he continued to pitch, he would ruin his arm — not just for baseball, but for everything. The doctors said that if he continued pitching, he might get to the point where he wouldn't even be able to lift his fork to his mouth.

Sandy pitched for one more year. Then, at the age of thirty, when he was at the peak of his talent, Sandy Koufax retired from baseball. He was the biggest star in the country. But he was also smart. He knew that he had a long life ahead of him. He wanted to live it as a whole person.

With four no-hitters and one perfect game, Sandy Koufax is still considered by many to be the greatest pitcher who ever lived.

HANK AARON'S 715th HOMERUN

Atlanta Braves vs. Los Angeles Dodgers
April 8, 1974

Hank Aaron hardly ever showed his feelings. He was a quiet man, who moved slowly. His teammates sometimes called him "Snowshoes," the way he pushed himself toward the plate. "Hank Aaron steps into the batting box as if he were going to sit down in it," wrote one writer. But inside that calm, slow-moving body was a power that drove pitchers crazy.

During the last game of one of Aaron's many seasons, a relief pitcher was called in. Aaron was to be his first batter. As the pitcher was warming up in fear of the mighty slugger, he thought to himself, "Suppose I never stop warming up; then I'll never have to pitch to Aaron." Relief pitchers are allowed to take as much time as they need to warm up.

"Suppose every time the umpire looks over to find out if I'm ready, I just shake my head, 'No, not yet.' Suppose I do that all night long. By about 10:30 in the morning, they'd probably give up and the season would be over."

Aaron had been in baseball for 21 years. And he had been doing that kind of thing to pitchers forever. With a whip of his bat, he would send balls flying out of stadiums.

For 21 years he had been building up his total of home runs — building toward one special night in Atlanta, Georgia. That night would be remembered forever by baseball fans as the night Hank Aaron broke Babe Ruth's home run record.

The week before, in Cincinnati, Aaron had tied the record with his 714th home run. Now, everyone was waiting for number 715. But the fans in Atlanta weren't exactly sitting around while they waited. The scene was like a carnival. The stands were jammed. 53,775 fans had come to witness the historic night. They were treated to a spectacular pre-game show. First, Aaron was paraded around the field through lines of majorettes as thousands of balloons flew off into the sky. Then came the "This Is Your Life, Hank Aaron" show.

The whole center field had been painted with a giant map of the United States in the shape of an American flag. Friends and relatives of Hank Aaron had been flown into Atlanta from all over the country to take part in the show. Movie stars were there. Famous singers were there. And even the governor of Georgia was there — a man named Jimmy Carter. A high school band played. A college choir sang. And Chief Noc-A-Homa, the Braves' mascot, did a dance with a flaming hoop.

Newspeople crowded around the star of the evening. Photographers snapped away. Aaron, the center of all the activity, barely showed any excitement. He was his usual unemotional self. He was a man with a job to do, and he just wanted the game to start so he could do it. He acted as though it was just another game.

But the Atlanta Braves' management knew that it wasn't just another game. They had been planning for this night for a long time. Ever since home run number 710, the management had been marking the balls with secret numbers in invisible ink. The ball that marked home run 715 was worth $25,000 to the fan who caught it, and the management didn't want thousands of fans showing up with fakes. The $25,000 would be given to the fan, but the ball would be presented to Aaron. Eventually, the ball would take its place in the Baseball Hall of Fame.

Fans knew that Aaron's long balls often came down in the left field stands. Thousands of fans, with visions of all that money in their heads, had crowded into the left field stands. They were wearing gloves and carrying nets. One fan showed up with a 15-foot bamboo pole with a fish net at the end. He had been practicing at home catching balls with it all winter long. Now, the big day was finally here.

A week earlier Aaron had smashed his first pitch of the season for home run number 714. Now the Atlanta Braves were on their home field. Everyone in the stands was hoping that Aaron would once again hit his first pitch out of the stadium. There was a hush when Aaron stepped into the batter's box at the beginning of the second inning. But the hush turned into boos when Al Downing, the Los Angeles pitcher, walked the slugger.

In the fourth inning Aaron came to bat again. The first pitch was a changeup. It hit the dirt in front of the plate. The umpire picked up the ball, turned it over, and threw it away. He called for another marked ball. Downing rolled the ball in his hand, then he stepped into position. The clock showed 9:07. Downing wound up and delivered a fastball. The stadium was silent as 53,775 fans heard the crack of the bat hitting the ball. And as Aaron raced toward first base, the ball arced toward the 385-foot sign in left-center field. As Aaron rounded the bases, the ball dropped into the Braves' bullpen. A roar went up from the crowd. A roar that lasted for ten minutes.

"It's gone! It's 715! There's a new home run champion," shouted the announcer, as Aaron shook hands with his father and hugged his mother.

The fans were still screaming when the Braves carried Aaron around the field. Fireworks shot into the sky behind center field.

Braves relief pitcher, Tom House, had been in the bullpen when Aaron hit the home run. Tom caught the ball and raced toward home plate with it. "The whole thing blew my mind," said Tom. "The ball came right at me, just rising off the bat on a line. If I'd frozen still like a dummy the ball would have hit me right in the middle of the forehead."

49

As a teammate and not a fan, House didn't get the $25,000. But he didn't care. "What made it worthwhile," he said, "was what I saw when I ran in with the ball, holding it in my gloved hand, running real fast... really just wanting to put it in Henry's hand. In that great crowd around home plate, I found him looking over his mother's shoulder, hugging her to him. And suddenly I saw what many people have never been able to see in him — deep emotion. I'd never seen that before. He has such cool. He never gets excited. He's so stable. And I looked and he had tears hanging on his lids. I could hardly believe it. 'Hammer, here it is,' I said. I put the ball in his hand. He said, 'Thanks kid,' and touched me on the shoulder."

And, while the millions of fans across the country were too far away to be touched by his hand, they were nonetheless teary-eyed and touched by the accomplishment of the great Hank Aaron.

PETE ROSE'S FORTY-FOUR-GAME
HITTING STREAK

Cincinnati Reds
June 14 — August 1, 1978

The summer of 1978 was exciting. Not because there were any moon shots. There weren't. And not because there were any earth-shaking, headline-grabbing events. That wasn't it at all. It was exciting because of Pete Rose, a big, brown-haired guy in a red hat and a white shirt.

Pete was the third baseman for the Cincinnati Reds. He was the kind of person that everybody liked. He was friendly. He was enthusiastic. He smiled a lot. He worked hard. And he was one terrific ballplayer.

Probably any ballplayer who got into a record-breaking hitting streak would excite our baseball-crazy country. Even if he were a grump. But the excitement in the summer of 1978 was especially enthusiastic because the ballplayer was Pete Rose.

When Pete started out in the minor leagues, he wasn't much of a ballplayer. "He can't make a double play. He can't throw, can't hit left-handed, and can't run." That was the report of Pete after his first minor league season in 1960.

Then how come he made it? Pete made it because he could hustle. Hustle means running full speed to first when you've drawn a walk or hit a blooper. Hustle means racing or diving or leaping to field a ball. Hustle means being in the right place at the right time. In his book, *Winning Baseball*, Pete wrote:

> Hustle means backing up a base. It means backing up your teammate. It means doing everything you can do to win a baseball game.

> Determination. That's what hustle is. If you aren't determined, you can't hustle. You must be determined to get the most out of yourself and your ability. You must be determined to win.

Pete's nickname was Charlie Hustle. He wasn't as fast, he wasn't as strong, and he wasn't as naturally talented as a lot of the stars in baseball. But in 1978, he was the most valuable player in the major leagues.

Pete was a good advertisement for hard work. "I've worked harder than the average guy because I've had to. I take twice as many ground balls as anybody before a game. I go out and I work and I work and I work."

In the summer of 1978, the whole country was out there with him. On June 14th, Pete had broken out of his worst batting slump ever with two hits against the Cubs. And then he just kept hitting — in game after game after game. By mid-July, newspapers across the country were printing little boxes with other people's streaks:

LONGEST STREAKS

Joe DiMaggio	1941	56
Willie Keeler	1897	44
Bill Dahler	1894	42
George Sisler	1922	41
Ty Cobb	1911	40
Tommy Holmes	1945	37

On July 25th, Cincinnati was in the Mets' Shea Stadium. Mets fans had filled the stands. They had come to watch Pete hit for the thirty-eighth straight game and pass Tommy Holmes' thirty-three-year-old modern National League record.

Just about every Met fan in the stadium was rooting for Pete to get a hit. "Do it, Pete" pennants were all over the stands. And hundreds of people wore T-shirts that said "I was there to see Pete do it. July 25, 1978." "Let's go, Pete. Let's go, Pete," chanted the fans.

Pete didn't make them wait very long. He smashed a single to left field in the third inning. The fans roared their support. Even Holmes was there to congratulate Pete. He was glad that someone like Pete had broken his record. "This is great for the millions of kids that play baseball," said Holmes. "Pete is a wonderful person."

Pete didn't stop with number 38. He kept going. He passed Ty Cobb and George Sisler and Bill Dahler. As the games piled up, so did the "Pete Rose fever." Wherever Pete went, the fans packed the ballparks. When the Reds visited Philadelphia, attendance went up an average of 11,000 per game. The people who ran the food and souvenir stands at Shea Stadium sent Rose a giant card of thanks for all the extra business they were getting because of his visits.

Everywhere Pete went, the fans cheered him on. He was under tremendous pressure. It was the kind of pressure that often made other players mean and surly. But not Pete. "I like pressure situations," he said. "They're fun. When people are urging me on, I can do things that are impossible."

People kept urging and Pete kept hitting. On August 1, in Atlanta, Pete tied Keeler's record of 44 straight hits. A crowd of 45,007 fans gave him a two-minute ovation when his bat connected with a fastball and gave him a single.

Fans across the country cheered along with the fans in the stands. Counting Pete's hits had become a national occupation. Everyone wanted to see Pete move past Joe DiMaggio's 56 hits. "I'm just starting," Pete had said when he passed Holmes. "I've got half the building up, and now I've got to build the rest."

But on August 2, in Atlanta, Pete went 0 for 4. The streak ended. There were tears across the country. Pete Rose, Charlie Hustle, had been a welcome guest in everyone's home. His 44 hits had been more than just hits. They were proof that hard work and determination could pay off.

People could identify with Pete Rose. Like them, he was an ordinary human being. If Pete could gain so much success through hard work, maybe they could too. Pete was an inspiration.

And that's why the summer of 1978 was exciting.

REGGIE JACKSON'S THREE HOME RUNS

World Series Final:
New York Yankees vs. Los Angeles Dodgers
October 18, 1977

Reggie Jackson wanted more than anything to do something spectacular in the World Series. All season people had been saying bad things about him. "He's overrated." "He's overpaid." "He has a big mouth." The press had said it. The fans had said it. Even his teammates had said it.

Ever since the day he had sat in a plush gold chair and signed his name on a three-million-dollar contract with the New York Yankees, he had been having problems. The other Yankees resented him. They were jealous when he got all that money. And they were even more jealous when he got all the attention.

There were times during spring training when it seemed as if Reggie was the only man on the team.

There they were — all the Yankees — among them superstars Chris Chambliss, Thurman Munson, Catfish Hunter—standing or sitting in front of their lockers talking to each other. And there was Reggie standing in front of his locker, surrounded by reporters. They were shouting questions at him, shoving microphones in his face. Reporters loved to interview Reggie. He always had controversial things to say. Controversial things make good news. "I am a surgeon," said Reggie one day. "I put on my glove and my hat and my shoes and I go out on the field, and I cut up the other team.... No one can quite do it the way I do."

The other Yankees tried not to listen. Baseball is a team sport, and it isn't a good idea to hate your teammate. But they heard and they resented. How could they not? One reporter wrote, "It's strange, a little dreamlike. Here is the superteam, but if this first week is an example, Reggie Jackson has taken over so totally that it's almost as if the other players are rookies who have yet to prove themselves to the press."

The resentment didn't go away once the season started. It got worse. Reggie liked to brag about how good he was. Sometimes he talked about how much better he was than his teammates. That's not a very good way to make friends.

When the 1977 season began, Reggie proved he

was right about how good he was. Time after time his powerful bat won games for the Yankees. And by the end of the season, Reggie Jackson had carried the Yankees into the World Series.

Reggie went into the World Series against the Dodgers determined to prove that he was more than just good. He wanted to prove that he was the best. He was going to show them all.

In the first game, Reggie knocked in the winning run. In the third game, he drove in one run and scored two. In game number four, Reggie's hits gave the Yankees their win. And in game number five, he drove in the final run.

But it was game number six that really proved what Reggie could do. In the fourth inning, with the Dodgers leading 3−2, and with Thurman Munson on base, Dodger pitcher threw Reggie a fastball for his first pitch. Reggie lined the ball into the right field seats. Head high, chest out, Reggie rounded the bases. Score: Yankees−4, Dodgers−3. When Reggie returned to the dugout, his teammates mobbed him.

The Dodgers changed pitchers. Reggie came to bat again in the fifth inning. Again there was a runner on base. And again Reggie slammed the first pitch—another fastball—into the right field stands. His teammates smothered him with slaps and pats and hugs. The fans roared. Reggie held up two

fingers in a victory sign for the photographers. The score was 7−3. But the game wasn't over.

Reggie was the leadoff batter in the eighth. A new pitcher was in. This time Reggie got a knuckle ball for his first pitch. The Dodgers didn't want to take any more chances with fastballs.

Reggie fired that first pitch into the air. It came down about 450 feet later in the center field stands. Score: 8−4. Three swings. Three home runs. In seventy-four years of World Series history, no one had ever done that. Babe Ruth had hit three home runs in a game in 1926 and again in 1928. But not three in a row.

The fans exploded. And so did Reggie's teammates. They swarmed all over him. They congratulated him. They pounded him on the back. Every one of them was glad Reggie Jackson was a Yankee. A lot of hard feelings are forgotten when the bragger delivers the goods. And Reggie Jackson had delivered.

Horse Racing

STEVE CAUTHEN AND AFFIRMED: A DYNAMITE DUO

The Belmont Stakes
June 10, 1978

"People say that Steve Cauthen is eighteen years old," said Laz Barrera, horse trainer. "For a while I believed them. But the more I watch him ride, the more I start to think other things. He must be at least one hundred years old, and maybe he don't come from Walton, Kentucky, at all.

"One night, when all the horse-racing world was sleeping, a small flying saucer landed out in the desert somewhere and he got off it. Stevie stands by the spaceship and waits three minutes. Horses come from everywhere toward the spaceship. They come out of California and Chicago and New York, and they line up and say, 'Stevie, come be my jockey.'

"Stevie doesn't say anything for a few minutes. Then he waves his hand for silence. 'Horses,' he says, 'I will get to you all eventually. Be patient. But now I am looking for a special horse; one that can win the Kentucky Derby. You there, big chestnut horse, what is your name?'

"This horse says, 'Affirmed.' And Stevie says, 'Affirmed, I choose you to be my first Derby winner. We will win in 1978 before a huge crowd. And I will put up a ride that people will talk about for years to come.'"

But Stevie was wrong. Oh, they won the Derby all right. But only one month later, *no one* was talking about it. Instead, they were talking about the "best durn horse race that's ever been run" — the Belmont Stakes of 1978.

Even before Belmont, the combination of Stevie Cauthen and Affirmed was magic. Stevie was the 5'1", 95-pound whirlwind who swept into jockeying when he was sixteen and showed the world of horse racing what the sport was all about. Stevie rode so low on his horses — to cut down on wind resistance — that other jockeys sometimes thought he had fallen off. "His back is always parallel to the ground," said one writer. "It looks as though a bowl of soup could be balanced there without ever losing a drop."

Affirmed was the dynamite horse who swept the 1978 Kentucky Derby and the Preakness with

Stevie on his back. In both races, the only competition had been a horse named Alydar. Now, the Belmont Stakes was about to begin. A victory at Belmont would earn for Affirmed and Stevie, the Triple Crown, horse racing's greatest honor.

Affirmed had lost only two times in his life—both times to Alydar at Belmont. "He's a great horse," said some about Affirmed. "But he can't go the distance." Belmont is a longer race than the other two.

"Anybody who thinks Affirmed can't run a distance is crazy," said his trainer, Barrera. "This horse can run five miles. He can beat Alydar with boxing gloves on his feet!"

There were no boxing gloves around, but there was a lot of tension on that beautiful, sunny day at Belmont Park. Every one of the 65,417 fans knew that Affirmed and his rider were trying to become the eleventh winners of the Triple Crown. And they all knew that Alydar had it in him to stop them.

As the horses were moved into the starting gate, Affirmed entered quietly. Alydar balked a little until he was in place. The gun went off.

The horses charged out of the gate. There were five horses maneuvering for position. But there were only two that mattered: Affirmed, with Stevie Cauthen attached to his back; and Alydar, with jockey Jorge Velasquez.

Stevie quickly edged Affirmed into the lead and next to the rail. It is an advantage in horse racing to run next to the rail because the inside circle around the track is shorter.

Once Stevie was set where he wanted to be, he slowed down. Velasquez slowed down too. Both jockeys knew that the last part of the race was going to be fast. They were pacing themselves.

By the end of the first half-mile, the two horses had pulled away from the rest of the pack—neck to neck. It was almost as if the riders and the horses had planned it that way. "I'll meet you at the half-mile mark," said Alydar. "Good idea," said Affirmed. "Let's give the folks a thrill." And they did.

The two horses raced as a team. For the final mile of the race, they were inches apart all the way. It was hard to see who was ahead. The movies show that Affirmed had a tiny edge.

As Affirmed and Alydar were rounding the last turn, with the finish line 3/16 of a mile away, it seemed to Stevie that Alydar was about to pull ahead. Stevie could feel that Affirmed was tired. He could feel it in the body of his horse. Stevie could feel the horse's moods as sharply as he could feel his own. He knew that something had to happen to give Affirmed the push to finish first.

With hands as smooth and quick as a magician's, Stevie switched his whip behind his back into his left hand. Stevie had ridden Affirmed dozens of times.

Never had he whipped him on the left side. Affirmed reacted. He pushed his nose up front and crossed the finish line first.

The fans exploded. Screams. Cheers. Tears. Hugs. They went wild. Never had two horses and two jockeys brought such beauty, such excitement, such skill to a horse race.

Stevie and Affirmed had run the fastest closing mile ever in the history of the Belmont race. (1:36 4/5).

They had run the most exciting mile ever. And, almost as an afterthought, they had captured the Triple Crown.

The little fellow from outer space and his magic horse had given racing fans the best horse race ever.

Olympics

BRUCE JENNER DOES IT ALL

Decathlon
Montreal, 1976

There have been faster runners than Bruce Jenner. There have been higher pole-vaulters. And longer jumpers. And better hurdlers. But for overall athletic ability, no one was better than Bruce Jenner when he went to the Montreal Olympics.

Bruce chose as his sport, the decathlon. Which is like saying that he chose to be good at everything. The decathlon is made up of ten different events. Together, the ten events are so demanding and so exhausting that they are run over a two-day period.

The first day's events are the 100-meter race, the long jump, the shot put, the high jump, and the 400-meter race. On the second day, the events are the 110-meter hurdles, the discus, the pole vault, the javelin, and the 1500-meter race. It's exhausting just to *read* the list.

Bruce competed in his first decathlon when he was in college in 1970. He liked it so much that he devoted the next six years of his life to becoming the best. Becoming the best at the decathlon means training endlessly. It means developing every muscle in your body — pushing your body until you can barely move.

With this kind of training, there is no time to relax. There's no time to earn a living. Bruce was 26 years old when he entered the 1976 Olympics in Montreal. At 26, most men are going to their offices or driving their trucks or teaching school. Bruce was still training.

At night, when most men were snuggled up in front of their television sets, Bruce was jumping over the hurdle he kept in the middle of his living room.

He trained seriously and long for the Montreal Olympics. He knew he had to be completely prepared. "Once I get to a meet," said Bruce, "The physical work is done. I wouldn't be there unless I was in good enough shape to win!" So Bruce trained six or seven hours a day.

"He's working on his technique constantly," said his wife, Chrystie, before the Olympics. "At the grocery store or at the bank, he's going through the motions of throwing the discus, or he's lifting his leg like he's hurdling. I'm sure people think he's crazy."

But after Montreal, no one thought he was crazy.

In the ten events, Bruce earned more points than anyone ever had. Coming into the last event — the 1500-meter race — Bruce knew that the gold medal was his. He had already earned enough points in the

other events. All he had to do was run the race safely and be sure that he crossed the finish line.

But Bruce wanted more. He wanted to finish the decathlon in record time. "It was my last meet," said Bruce. "And I wanted a world record."

To get that record, Bruce had to run all-out. He had to run the race faster than he ever had. 1500 meters is long. Athletes who don't pace themselves run the risk of collapsing before they finish.

As Bruce began the first lap, he could hear the crowd cheering him on. He moved faster with every stride. "The more I picked up the pace," he said, "the better it felt. I couldn't have slowed down if I had wanted to. At the end I looked at the clock and saw I had the record. It was the happiest day of my life."

Bruce had set his goal at 8,600 points. He ended up with 8,618. The papers called him "the greatest athlete in the world."

In the next years, the name Bruce Jenner would become known all over the world. His face would appear in television commercials. His warm, friendly smile and his floppy brown hair would be recognized everywhere. Companies would ask Bruce to help them sell their products.

Finally — at the age of 26 — Bruce Jenner was ready to sit back and let all those years of hard work pay off in profits. But all the profits would never give him the thrill he felt when he looked up at the clock and discovered that he was "the greatest athlete in the world."

NADIA COMANECI WINS THE WORLD

Gymnastics
Montreal, 1976

There was a hush in the giant gymnastics hall in Montreal. A tiny wisp of a girl, eighty-five pounds and less than five feet tall, stepped up to the uneven parallel bars. Her soft, brown hair was tied back with white and red ribbons. Her dark eyes were intense with concentration; her face, expressionless. As she stood before the bars in her white leotard, her tiny body was, for a second, a sculpted statue, each muscle magnificently molded.

Then, with an explosion of energy, Nadia Comaneci rocketed onto the bars. As 18,000 people in the stadium gasped, the tiny body twirled, twisted, flew around the bars with such incredible control and such daring that *Newsweek* magazine would later call her performance, "near miraculous."

It was as though she were one of those toy monkeys that is attached to a little trapeze. When you squeeze the handle, the monkey spins around. But toy monkeys can't move from bar to bar. And they can't hold themselves suspended in the air the way Nadia could. And until that moment in the 1976 Olympics, neither could any human being.

For her final dismount from the uneven parallel bars, Nadia performed a move that is now known as the "Salto Comaneci." While the world audience looked on in amazement, Nadia released the upper bar moving forward, did a half twist, then changed directions and finished with a back somersault.

No one had ever seen a performance like it. Every muscle of her tiny body had been in perfect control. Nadia burst into smiles as she greeted the thrilled cheers, both arms in the air in triumph.

Even the Olympic judges were astounded by the flawless performance. Every finger, every toe, every movement of the tiny, twisting body had been perfect. They could find no flaws. For the first time in the history of Olympic gymnastics, the judges awarded a perfect score of 10.

Later, Nadia approached the beam with the same confidence she had shown on the bars. As her tiny body sprang from the beam into the air, she seemed to be flying. As she landed on the four-inch beam, she was secure and graceful and fearless.

When Nadia ended her bar routine with a double-twisting dismount, the audience jumped to their feet, roaring their excitement. Again, the judges awarded her a 10. In all, Nadia collected a total of seven perfect scores which earned her three

gold medals, a silver medal, and a bronze. Little Nadia had swept the Olympics.

Nadia was small only in size. Her talents were enormous, and she had been developing those talents since she was six years old. When she was still in kindergarten, she had been chosen to attend a special school for gymnasts.

Nadia lived in a small town in Romania with her mother, her father, and her brother. One day a gymnastics teacher came to Nadia's house. He had seen Nadia on the school playground. He had watched her doing pretend-gymnastics. He liked what he saw. So he asked Nadia's parents if she could come to his school to learn gymnastics. Nadia's parents were very proud to send her to the gymnastics school where, they knew, young girls were trained to become champions.

In the school, Nadia worked hard. And she loved it. From the very beginning, Nadia performed with an energy and an enthusiasm that set her apart from the other girls. The first time Nadia stepped on the beam, she was relaxed and comfortable. Most people are frightened to even walk on the beam. But Nadia was fearless. "I have never been afraid," she told reporters in Montreal.

Nadia worked many hours in the school gym, building the muscles that would enable her body to do the difficult movements of the gymnastics routines. She did push-ups and knee-bends and chin-ups. She spent hour after hour with her instructors doing exercises and splits and jumps and leaps.

At the age of seven, Nadia finished thirteenth in the Romanian National Junior Championships. The next year, she came in first. She won the Cup of

Europe when she was thirteen and the American Cup in 1976. In Montreal, at the age of fourteen, Nadia had her finest moment. She dazzled the world with her feats. "A Star is Born" said the headline in one magazine. And magazines all over the world were printing her picture and writing her story.

When Nadia returned to Romania, she was greeted at the airport by thousands of people. They gave her flowers and welcomed her home with signs. The tiny girl with the brown ponytail had given pride to her nation. And she had earned the respect of the entire world.

MARK SPITZ COLLECTS SEVEN GOLD MEDALS

Swimming
Munich, 1972

Every four years the Olympics are held in a different country. But it doesn't matter where they are held. For every young athlete, the road to the Olympics is long and hard.

Mark Spitz began the trip when he was two years old. His family lived in Hawaii. Every day Mark's mother took him to Waikiki Beach. "You should have seen little Mark dash into the water," said Mrs. Spitz. "That little boy would run like he was trying to commit suicide. He loved the water."

But lots of kids love the water and they never make it to the Olympics. One reason is that they probably don't have fathers like Mr. Spitz. Mark's father wanted Mark to be a champion. "Swimming isn't everything," Mr. Spitz used to say. "Winning is."

Over and over Mr. Spitz used to impress upon his son the importance of winning. Often when they were standing at the edge of a swimming pool, Mr. Spitz would point to the racing lanes and ask, "Mark, how many lanes in the pool?" Mark would count the lanes and answer his father. "And how many of those lanes win?" Mr. Spitz would ask. "One," the little boy would say. And Mark knew that if he wanted to be a winner, *he* had to be in that lane. At an age when most little boys were happy to be building with blocks, Mark was dreaming of winning the Olympics.

By the time Mark was eight, he was racing on a swim team. By the time he was nine, he was training four days a week. "During those workouts," said Mark, "I'd come out of the pool and I'd be pooped and I'd gasp, 'How much time do I have before I have to swim again?' And the coach would say, 'Ten seconds — ready, set, jump in.' He made me work hard and he gave me a competitive urge, but it was fun, too."

Hard work and a strong desire to win. Those are two of the main ingredients of a champion. Mark had both. When Mark was 10 years old he set his first United States record. He swam the 50-yard butterfly in 31 seconds.

By the time Mark was fourteen, he was training by 6:30 every morning. And often he would be back in the pool in the afternoon. When he was seventeen, Mark set world records in the 400-meter freestyle, the 100-meter butterfly, the 200-meter butterfly, and the 110-meter butterfly. That year he was selected as the world's "Swimmer of the Year."

It was nice to be "Swimmer of the Year," but Mark's real goal was to be an Olympic champion. The closer he got to the 1968 Olympics, the harder he worked. In the spring of 1968, Mark swam every morning before school and for two more hours after school.

Mark's coach was very confident about Mark's chances of winning in the Olympics. Mark had a smooth, easy, powerful stroke. "Mark is loose and long-muscled," said his coach. "The way he slips through the water is simply mystifying."

One of the reason's for Mark's easy glide through the water was that his arms were extra-long from his shoulder to his elbow. That gave him a longer pull on his strokes. Mark was also able to bend his legs forward at the knees. That gave him extra power in his kick.

By the time Mark arrived at the 1968 Mexico City Olympics, he was sure he was going to win. Mark bragged to the newspapers that he would win six gold medals. No one had *ever* won more than five. All the papers printed Mark's prediction. People thought it was absurd for an eighteen-year-old kid to make a boast like that. Even his teammates resented him for being such a braggart.

Mark was very nervous when the races began. He ended up winning only two gold medals—as part of relay teams. He didn't win any in the individual events. Many people—including some of his teammates—laughed at him. They were happy he had lost. He had bragged too much.

Mark left Mexico City disappointed. One reporter said that Mark "retreated like a wounded shark." People were laughing at him now, but Mark made up his mind that they wouldn't be laughing after the next Olympics.

Mark spent the next four years in college at the University of Indiana. He trained and raced with the Indiana swim team. By the summer of 1971, Mark was older, stronger, and smarter than he had been in Mexico. He weighed 170 pounds, and he stood six feet tall. That summer he swam an average of four-and-a-half hours and 8,500 yards a day. "I'm in my best condition ever," he said. "Mentally as well as physically. I don't get nervous any more. Now when I get up on the starting blocks, I stay calm. Everything about my swimming feels just great."

By August of the next summer, Mark was ready for the 1972 Olympics in Munich, Germany. This time around, Mark didn't make any predictions. "I'll just try to do the best I can," he told the news-people.

It turned out that Mark Spitz's best was the best ever. Mark put on a spectacular show for the entire Olympic-watching world. He began the show with the 200-meter butterfly. As he stepped up on the starting block, Mark was a different person than he had been in Mexico City. He was totally confident and sure of his skills. When the smiling, dripping Mark climbed out of the pool after the race, he was the winner of the gold medal and a world record. Thirty minutes later, he won his second gold medal with the United States 400-meter relay team.

The next day Mark raced in the 200-meter free-style. At first he trailed his teammate, Steve Genter. Then, with his large hands and his forceful stroke, Mark caught up and passed him. Gold medal number three and another world record.

Two days later Mark whipped through the 100-meter butterfly for another record and another

medal. And then he set another record with the 800-meter freestyle relay team. Mark was now tied for the record of most Olympic medals in one year—five. Suddenly, the world took notice of the young man they had laughed at in Mexico.

Crowds followed Mark down the street. People stopped him for his autograph. Mark loved the attention. All those years of training were finally paying off. "When you walk into a restaurant with Mark Spitz," said one of his teammates, "you can bet they'll wait on you!"

There were 4,000 newspeople in Munich to cover the Olympics. They all wanted to talk to Mark. "Just five minutes," they all said. If Mark had talked to them all, he'd have been in Munich all winter.

Newspeople, audiences, fans around the world, everyone was talking about Mark Spitz. Even the other athletes wanted to be near him. They wanted to touch him. Maybe some of his success would rub off.

Mark wanted to sit back and enjoy his fame. But there was still more business. Two more races. As Mark stepped onto the starting block to race the 100-meter freestyle, the whole world was watching. This was Mark's weakest event, but he was fired with the passion to win that his father had given him. Mark dived into the water and shot to the front. Arm after arm, he slipped through the water with astonishing force. He reached the 50-meter turn in record time, and he forged ahead. When Mark's hand hit the finish line, he had another medal and another record — six of each.

Now there was only one event left — the 400-meter medley-relay. Mark wanted more than anything to win it. "I can't tell you how much this means to me. I just don't want to lose."

And, of course, he didn't. When his last race was over, Mark had his seventh gold medal and his seventh record.

The Olympics had never seen anything like it. His teammates hoisted him on their shoulders. The applause was like thunder. And as Mark sat there grinning and holding out his seventh gold medal, all the work, the hours of training, the pain of pushing his body to its limits — all the steps on that long, hard road to the Olympics—faded into nothing. All he could hear were the cheers. And all he could feel was the thrill of knowing that he was the best.

TEAM AMERICA'S DREAM COMES TRUE

Hockey
Lake Placid, 1980

It was an impossible dream—a USA gold medal in hockey. But 20 guys on skates with hockey sticks in their hands and USA shirts on their backs couldn't get that dream out of their heads.

The reason it seemed an impossible dream was because the United States' team was young and inexperienced. Many of them were college students still in their teens. Their European opponents were older, more experienced and, overall, better hockey players.

If, by some quirk of luck Team America could win through the early games, they would still have to beat the Russian team. That team had not lost an

Olympic hockey game in twelve years. There was no way the college kids could conquer the "best hockey team in the world." In fact, the U.S. team had already lost to the Russians — 10–3 — just three days before the Olympics opened. One sportswriter had headlined a pre-Olympic article, "Please...Nobody Tell the U.S. Hockey Team It Has No Chance."

But the U.S. hockey team didn't care what anybody was saying. They were young, enthusiastic, and bursting with optimism.

With a massive dose of confidence and extraordinary skill, they tied Sweden and then went on to beat Czechoslovakia, Norway, and West Germany. After every game, the boys on Team America hooted and hollered and hugged each other. They danced around the stadium with big smiles on their faces. And when they left the stadium, they were cheered by the crowds, mostly Americans, who had caught their enthusiasm. By the time the USA team played the Russians, they were skating on air.

The Russian game was a major event not only in Lake Placid, but in living rooms and restaurants all over the country — everywhere people could get close to a television set. The game was viewed as a lot more than a sporting event. The United States and Russia were having political problems. A U.S. hockey victory would be seen by many as not just a victory for the 20-member team—but as a victory for our country and our way of life.

Families gathered in front of television sets to watch. Neighbors assembled so they could cheer their team together. One group of teenagers in Los Angeles had a game-watching party where every guest had to bring "something American." They came with hot dogs and baseball bats, apple pies, and American flags, Chevrolets and political bumper stickers. One boy even brought his Mom.

In Lake Placid on the day of the game, people were paying as much as $350.00 for tickets to the match. And they all got their money's worth.

In the first period, U.S. goalie, Jim Craig, made 16 saves—but he gave up two goals. At the end of the second period, the Americans were losing, 3–2. When the third and final period began, the fans in the stands were frenzied. "USA! USA! USA! USA!" they shouted. American flags were waving furiously. An extra charge for the already highly charged team.

These kids who "didn't have a chance" burst into the third period determined to skate away with another victory. At 8:39 of the third period, Mark Johnson tied the game. Then, team captain Mike Eruzione exploded the puck past the Russian goalie and the impossible happened.

"Do you believe in miracles?" asked Al Michaels

before the game was over. And, as the final buzzer sounded, score USA 4, Russians 3, he shouted the answer, "YES!" And the whole country rejoiced with him.

The Lake Placid fans went crazy. They celebrated all night long. But not the hockey players. They still had one game to go — against Finland — before they could collect their gold medals.

"To be one game away from the gold medal is the dream of a lifetime," said forward John Harrington. "There was no way we were going to blow it."

And, of course, they didn't.

USA was trailing 1−0 at the end of the first period. Then, 4½ minutes into the second period, they tied the score. Two minutes later, Finland scored again and the 2−1 score held until the last period. But no one gave up.

Team America had proven itself a team that could come from behind. It had trailed Sweden and then tied them up in the last 27 seconds. It had trailed Czechoslovakia before beating them 7−3. It had trailed Norway 1−0 at the start of that contest and ended up winning 5−1. Against West Germany, the United States had come from behind to win 4−2. And in the Soviet game, USA had trailed the Russians three times before winning.

So, the flags kept waving, the chants kept coming, and the U.S. hockey team began picking up goals. "We want gold. We want gold. We want gold," the fans yelled. USA responded by tying the score 2−2. "We want gold. We want gold. We want gold." Another goal. USA 3, Finland 2.

The tension built to unbearable when, in the final minutes of the game, the Americans were called for three penalties. But the Finns were unable to score.

Then, with 3½ minutes to play, Johnson scored the final goal of the game. The USA had won the gold.

Every city in the country cheered them. President Carter called to offer his congratulations. Sports fans were shaking with excitement. Many of the newscasters would later claim that winning the hockey gold medal in Lake Placid was the most thrilling sports moment they had ever experienced.

And it all happened because 20 young men had an impossible dream.

Basketball

THE COURAGE OF WILLIS REED

NBA Final: New York Knicks vs. Los Angeles Lakers
May 8, 1970

In one game, early in the season, Willis Reed, captain of the New York Knicks, saw the ball headed out of bounds. He ran across the court, threw himself at the ball, and hit it to one of his teammates. The ball went in — but Willis went out. His huge, 6'10", 245-pound body sailed into the second row of seats and crashed into the wooden chairs. No one but Willis was hurt. The next day, his body was covered with bruises. His left hand, which he had landed on, was swollen and taped. His pinky was dislocated.

The Knicks coach had called a practice for that day. But there was no game that night, so the coach had told the team that they didn't have to come if they didn't want to. Willis Reed, bandaged hand and bruised body, showed up. "Why?" someone asked. "Why didn't you just stay home and heal?" "If there's a practice," said Willis, "and the captain doesn't go, why should anybody else?"

Willis Reed was that kind of guy.

Willis gave every inch of himself. "It's a shame," he used to say, "if you don't get the most of your potential. It's a shame if a man doesn't hustle. That hurts. It hurts when you see a guy who does not do what he can do."

Willis did everything he could do — and more. Once he had been an awkward ninth grader in Bernice, Louisiana. He could barely handle the ball. Sometimes his body seemed to go in 10 different directions at the same time. But Willis wanted to play. He pushed himself. He began to jump rope to help his body move smoothly. He practiced shooting. He dribbled endlessly. Before long, Willis was an all-state player.

Willis never stopped pushing himself. He pushed in his early years as a New York Knick. And when he was made captain of the Knicks, he pushed even harder — both on and off the court.

On the court, Willis was like an octopus. He

blocked shots, batted down passes, and waved his arms as though he had eight of them. Offensively, he consistently totalled up more points than anyone else on the team. At center, Willis battled men much taller than he. And he won.

Off the court, Willis was a solid, intelligent, strong leader. He was always fair in his dealings with the team. There was no superstar treatment on his team, no privileged players. They were all Knicks.

The Knicks were a crazy, wonderful, devoted family in the 1969–1970 season. A winning family. And they all knew that Willis was the key to their success in making it all the way to the NBA finals against the Los Angeles Lakers.

In the 24 years that the NBA and the Knicks had been in existence, the Knicks had never won a title. They had not even been in the finals since 1953. The Lakers, on the other hand, had played in seven finals in the last nine years.

Before the opening game of the four-out-of-seven match for the championship, everyone wondered how Willis Reed and the Lakers' superstar center, Wilt Chamberlain, would match up against each other. It was Willis's job to keep Chamberlain in check.

After the first game, the wondering was over. Willis handled Chamberlain with ease. The Knicks won the first game and Willis was high scorer with 37 points.

In the second game, Chamberlain came to life. The Lakers won in overtime. By the fifth game, each team had won twice.

Game five was in New York. After only eight minutes, the Lakers had a 10-point lead. But early scoring doesn't mean much in basketball, so New York wasn't worried. During the match, Willis had been able to contain Chamberlain. That's what counted. Then, as Willis dribbled down the court for a lay-up, he twisted and faked in an effort to get past Chamberlain. But suddenly Willis was on the floor, writhing in pain.

Madison Square Garden became silent. "Oh, my goodness," thought Dave DeBusschere, the Knicks' big forward.

"It's all over," thought Willis, as he felt the searing pain shoot up his hip. "We've gone so far and it's all over."

The doctor helped Willis into the dressing room and examined him. Willis had strained the rectus femoris muscle in his right hip. That's the muscle that lifts up the leg every time a person takes a step. The doctor sent word out to the floor, "He's through for the night."

At the half, the score was 53–40, Los Angeles. As the Knicks walked into the locker room, it seemed as though something had been torn out of each of them. Their captain was finished. He was their strength. In that one twisting moment on the floor, it seemed as though the Knicks had come apart.

During the half-time break, Red Holzman, the Knicks' coach, worked out a strategy for playing without Willis. Then, just as the team was returning to the floor, Holtzman said one last thing. "Let's win this one for Willis. He's won a lot of games for us, let's win one for him." And the Knicks went back out there determined.

While Willis lay on the long table in the dressing room listening to the game, the Knicks made a fantastic comeback. They won the game for Willis, 107 to 100.

The next day the Knicks flew to Los Angeles for game number six. Willis went too. He could barely walk. He couldn't climb steps. The doctor and the trainer went with Willis to the hotel health club. Willis spent hours alternating ice and heat on his hip. Maybe, they hoped, the hot and cold treatment would ease the pain and allow him to play that night. The decision was up to the doctor. Everyone agreed on only one thing: if playing was going to cause permanent damage, Willis should not play.

After hours of treatment, Willis was able to walk. But the doctor decided that there was a possibility of further injury. Willis did not play in game six.

The final score of the game was 135–113, Lakers. Chamberlain had piled up 45 points. Game score: 3–3. The next game would be the last. Everyone flew to New York for game number seven.

Just before he left, Willis made a promise to his teammates. "Don't worry," he told them. "I'm playing that seventh game even if I don't have any legs, even if I have to crawl out there."

That night, Willis's old college coach called him on the phone. "You've got to be out there when they throw that ball up," the coach said. "If you've got an ounce of breath in you, you've got to be out there." Nobody had to give Willis a pep talk. He had already made up his mind.

The next day Willis came early to Madison Square Garden. When his trainer and the doctor had finished working on his hip, they wanted to watch him on the court. Willis put on a uniform and walked, in pain, to the court. Slowly, he worked out, throwing soft one-handers into the basket. Every step was agony. But Willis's face showed no pain. Willis had spotted Chamberlain standing just off court. Willis refused to give the slightest hint to Chamberlain that there was a problem. When they returned to the dressing room, the doctor decided that he would let Willis play.

A few hours later, every fan in Madison Square Garden stared in anticipation as the players came onto the floor from the locker rooms. One by one the Knicks jogged onto the floor. Bill Bradley, Dave DeBusschere, Cazzie Russell. One after another the Knicks began working out. Willis was missing. The fans sank into their seats. The Knicks couldn't do it without Willis. They had worked so hard all season. They had come so far. And now, to end the season this way....

Then suddenly, a figure appeared on the floor. The fans exploded. Willis was back in uniform! He was going to play!

The Knicks beamed with confidence. Willis was back. He really *was* going to play. Meanwhile, the Lakers had a less enthusiastic look on their faces.

When the game began, Willis was in pain. But he knew what he had to do. "I went out to try to contain Wilt, if possible, on one leg," Willis said later. "I was determined that he wouldn't score the way he did in the sixth game."

After the tip-off, Willis moved downcourt, dragging his leg. He took the ball and shot a soft one-hander. Two points. The crowd nearly knocked the roof off the Garden. A few minutes later, Willis shot another one from just outside the foul circle. Basket. The crowd exploded again.

With those two shots, Willis Reed was sending out a message. "I can do it," he said to his team-mates. "If I can do it so can you."

And the Knicks relaxed. Willis was back. They could work around him. They could work with him.

Willis's message to the Lakers was different. "Don't write me off," he said, "I'm still a threat." And the Lakers felt threatened.

"What courage," thought Bill Bradley. "What dedication to the team." The Knicks knew that Reed was in pain. The muscle in his right leg was barely able to hold him up. Once during the game it gave way, and Willis folded onto the floor. The Knicks called a time-out and sat Willis down for a few minutes. But he was up again after the time-out.

The courage and inspiration of Willis Reed drove the Knicks. Willis played for a total of 27 minutes. His first two shots were the only two he made. But his presence on the floor, the knowledge that he was there if they needed him, was enough to give the Knicks the confidence they needed. The final score was 113—99, Knicks. The Knicks were the NBA Champions for the first time in 24 years!

At the end of the game Cazzie Russell was asked how his team had done it. "It was Willis," he said. "His mere presence, the way he kept going, the way he kept moving Wilt, forcing him further out. The captain showed me something. He showed every-

body something. He showed he has a lot of guts. . . .
We looked at him, hurting, and he's still going up
and down that court, still banging with Wilt and I
know it made us all play harder. I know it made us
all think, if he can do it, the way he's hurting, then
we can all do a little bit more."

Willis Reed was that kind of guy.

Soccer

PELÉ'S LAST GAME:
A GREAT MAN SAYS GOOD-BYE

New York Cosmos vs. Santos of Brazil
October 1, 1978

They were too poor to buy a ball. They were even too poor to buy shoes. So the barefoot boys in the small Brazilian city of Bauru made their own soccer "ball." They stuffed rags and paper into an old sock and tied it up. And all day long they kicked the sock around in the street. By the end of the day the battered sock was crumbled. The next day, the boys stuffed another sock. Pelé still remembers his angry father shouting, "Where did my other sock go?"

When he wasn't kicking a sock around the street, Edson Arantes do Nascimento, known as Pelé, was bouncing a grapefruit around the house. He was bouncing it with his head, his feet, his shoulders, his knees.

By the time he was 10, Pelé knew that soccer would be his life. "I was born for soccer, just as Beethoven was born for music," he said later. He dropped out of school at the end of fourth grade and practiced soccer. When he was fifteen, Pelé began his career as a professional soccer player.

When it ended, 22 years later, Pelé was acclaimed as king of the world's most popular game. He had scored twice as many goals as his nearest challenger — a total of 1,281. He had thrilled fans in 88 countries with his magic combination of speed and ball control, and with his brilliant ability to anticipate where the ball would be.

Pelé's skills as a player were unbelievable. He could glide through packs of opponents with the grace of a dancer, the power of a leopard. He would appear in one spot, then almost instantly in another, then in a third place, almost as if he had superhuman powers to materialize and dematerialize whenever he wanted. Pelé could dribble the ball down the field with such speed and beauty, it looked as though the ball were attached to his leg by a rubber band. And he could pass like no one else.

Thousands of stories were written about Pelé, but rarely did the writers compare him to other players. Pelé was so extraordinary that he could not be compared. "Pelé," said one writer, "was simply a genius, a marvelous union of brain and muscle."

But as brilliant as Pelé was on the soccer field, his playing skills were only part of his genius. Pelé was also a fine, generous, warm person. The highest-paid sports figure in the world, and a multimillionaire, Pelé always had time for kindness. He would sign autographs until he could barely move his arm. He would talk to strangers as though they were friends. Often, he would travel around the world to hold soccer clinics for young people.

Thousands of children have learned soccer from the great, and humble, Pelé.

He earned the respect of kings and queens and heads of state. When Pope Paul VI met Pelé he said, "Don't be nervous, my son. I am more nervous than you because I have been wanting to meet Pelé personally for a long time." In the early 1970's, the war in Biafra was stopped for two days because both sides wanted to see Pelé play.

In 1974 Pelé retired. He had played his entire professional career with the Santos of Brazil. Other countries had wanted him to play for them. But Brazil had declared that Pelé was a "national treasure" that couldn't be exported.

Pelé was indeed a treasure. And in 1975, after his retirement, Brazil at last agreed to share him with the United States. Pelé agreed to put on the uniform of the New York Cosmos because he wanted to make soccer a popular sport in the United States. It was already the most popular sport in the rest of the world.

As a Cosmo, Pelé traveled all over the country. People who had barely heard of soccer came to see the great Pelé play. Soon, schools and playgrounds in every state were offering soccer in their athletic programs. By October 1, 1978, Pelé had accomplished his goal. The Cosmos' general manager said, "United States soccer went from the Stone Age to the Jet Age in one jump when Pelé arrived."

So, with his mission accomplished, Pelé decided once again to retire. On a rainy day in October, in New Jersey's Giants Stadium, Pelé played his last game.

The Cosmos had invited the Santos, Pelé's team in Brazil, to play in this last game. Pelé was going to play the first half of the game with the Cosmos and the second half of the game with the Santos. When the game was over, he would retire as a member of the team he had started with in 1956.

In the first half of the game, while Pelé was wearing his Cosmos shirt, the Cosmos were awarded a free kick, thirty yards from the Santos goal. Pelé took the kick. He blasted it into the net, right past the sprawling, fallen Santos goalie. The crowd cheered.

At halftime, Pelé removed his Cosmos shirt with the number 10 across the back. He waved it at the

crowd and handed it to his father. Then he put on his number 10 Santos shirt.

At the end of the game, Pelé removed his Santos shirt and handed it to his first coach. As the crowd shouted, "Pelé, Pelé, Pelé," he ran a victory lap around the field. When he returned, he was lifted onto the shoulders of two of his Cosmo teammates and carried off the field.

"Now that he is gone," said one avid soccer fan, "part of my blood is gone. He has taken with him part of the heart of all the people in the world who love soccer."

But the man was wrong. Pelé had not taken; he had given. He had given excitement, and love to people around the world. "My greatest hope," Pelé said when he first came to the United States, "is that someday all humankind... will join hands and become brothers."

Pelé helped the world toward that goal. In his speech before the 76,000 fans who had come to see his last game, Pelé said, "Ladies and gentlemen, I am very happy to be here with you in this greatest moment of my life. I want to thank you all, every single one of you. I want to take this opportunity to ask you to pay attention to the young of the world, the children, the kids. We need them too much. And I want to ask you to please say with me, three times — love! love! love!"

And as the 75,646 persons repeated the word, Pelé cried. His wife and father joined him on the floor. They held him closely and cried with him.

Pelé has said, "Through simplicity and sincerity, you can put all humankind together." He has tried to do just that.

Hockey

THE BOBBY ORR SHOW

Stanley Cup Final:
Boston Bruins vs. New York Rangers
May 11, 1972

"The way I saw it," said one of the Boston Bruins after the game, "Bobby controlled the puck for forty minutes and was nice enough to let the other 35 players in the game use it for the other 20 minutes. He's not a selfish kid, you know."

It was a one-man show. The place was Madison Square Garden in New York City. There were some other players on the ice. Some of them skated around in uniforms that told the fans they were on a team called the New York Rangers. They were good skaters. Maybe they should have gotten jobs with an ice show.

The other people playing on the ice were the Boston Bruins, Bobby Orr's team. They could have been down the street watching a Broadway show.

Bobby would have won without them. Madison Square Garden had called it the sixth game of the 1972 Stanley Cup playoffs. They should have called it the Bobby Orr Show. "The guy had it," said the captain of the Rangers. "And when he had it, there wasn't a thing we could do about it."

Bobby Orr had *always* had it — from the first minute he put skates on his feet. "He was the only kid who could raise the puck as if he was born to raise pucks," said one of those who played with Bobby in Parry Sound, Ontario, a small town in Canada. "He once fired a wrist-shot from the blue line that went in the net over the goalie's shoulder. He was eight years old."

The kid was a terror on the ice. He drove the coaches of opposing teams to babble like baboons. Once, an opposing coach was trying to fire up his team before a game with Bobby's team. He held up a piece of paper on which Bobby had signed his name. Bobby was just learning how to write in school. "Look at this scrawl!" said the coach. "Look at the way he signs his name! He can't even write properly. Look at it. Look at this chicken scratching! How can a kid who can't even sign his name play hockey? He *can't*, that's what, he *can't!*"

But he could, that's what, he could! Bobby soon became known all over Canada as the kid-genius on ice. One day when Bobby was 12 years old, scouts for the Boston Bruins came into town. As they watched Bobby move the puck and fly across the ice, they were amazed. They had never seen such skill in someone so young. The scouts rushed back to Boston "uttering sounds," said one journalist, "like Columbus sighting America for the first time."

The scouts talked to the management. The management listened, wide-eyed. *The Boston Bruins signed Bobby Orr when he was twelve years old.*

Bobby played on Bruin farm teams until he was eighteen. And then, in 1966, he glided into Boston with his magic stick. From day one Bobby Orr took over the city. Boston hadn't had a good team for more than 20 years. The fans had been waiting for Bobby. They knew he was going to bring them glory.

In his first season with the Bruins, Bobby scored 13 goals and made 28 assists. He received the Calder Trophy as Rookie-of-the-Year. And he was named to the second All-Star Team. In his first year! A few years later, Bobby brought the Stanley Cup back to Boston.

Bobby became the idol of every fan in New England. There were Bobby Orr parades and Bobby Orr parties. Bobby received more birthday cards than the President of the United States. It was even rumored that Bobby received more Christmas cards than Santa Claus. Every day his poor postman carted 5,000 letters. "This is Orr country," said millions of bumper stickers. And experts proclaimed that Bobby could do more with his stick and his skates than any player in hockey history.

So, really, no one was very surprised in New York City that day when—practically by himself—Bobby Orr once again brought the Stanley Cup to the Bruins. In the first period, Orr fired a low, hard shot 35 yards into the net for the first score. In the second period, when Boston had to play with one and then two men in the penalty box, Bobby played a game of keep-away-the-puck. He would get the puck behind his net and move it slowly up to the center. Then he would turn around and go back to his net again. The Rangers tried desperately to get their sticks on the puck, but there was no way. When they closed in, Bobby would shoot the little round thing all the way to the end of the rink.

The second goal of the game came when Bobby passed the puck to a teammate. The puck bounced off the teammate's skate, hit a post, and landed in the goal. He couldn't have planned it that way. But with Bobby Orr, you never knew. Bobby allowed one of his teammates to make the final goal and Boston skated off with the Stanley Cup. Orr had hypnotized the Rangers. "We were lucky to get out alive," said one of them.

But they did. Alive and whole and healthy. Most

of them, much healthier than Bobby. Bobby had played all six of the playoff games in terrible pain. His left knee had been a problem for a number of years. He had had two operations on it in 1967. Now, it was troubling him again.

"How's your knee?" asked one of his teammates before the game.

"I feel fine, just fine," answered Orr. "There's nothing wrong with me."

As he was saying the words, his trainer was wrapping a bandage around his knee. Several times during the 1972 Stanley Cup games Bobby had had to go into the dressing room to have ice taped to his knee and bandage wrapped around the tape.

"He was playing hurt," said the Ranger coach. "Real hurt. And it was so obvious. But he did the job and won for the Bruins. I wish I was hurt like that."

Probably if the coach had been given the opportunity to switch places, he wouldn't have done it. Over the next five seasons Bobby had more and more problems with his knee. He had four more operations. And still he continued to play — winning awards, but torturing himself.

In 1977, Orr was asked, "Aren't you ruining your knee by playing on it?" "The knee is already permanently damaged," said Bobby. "It can't get much worse than it is by another year or two of playing.... There are certain things I won't be able to do anymore. I can't run. I can't play tennis..."

"Why?" asked the press, his fans, his family. Why did he keep playing all those years as his knee continued to get worse?

"Bobby," said one journalist, "you're wealthy. There are no more prizes to win. Why do you keep playing? Why do you keep putting yourself through this?"

"You must understand," was the answer. "It's very difficult to just sit and watch and not be able to take part in something that you love so much. It's very, very difficult."

In 1978, at the age of thirty, Bobby officially retired. "I worked hard," he said. "But I now know for sure that my leg cannot handle playing."

Even with such a young retirement, Bobby had

shown more skills and given more thrills to hockey fans than anyone else in history. He had spent most of his young life doing the thing he most loved to do. Bobby Orr had no regrets.

Tennis

"LITTLE" TRACY AUSTIN COMES OF AGE

The United States Open — 1979
September 9, 1979

On September 9, 1979, 16-year-old Tracy Austin left tennis fans everywhere with their mouths hanging open. On that day Tracy became the youngest champion — male or female — in the history of the U.S. Open at Forest Hills, New York.

Tracy didn't just pop up out of nowhere at age 16. But her tremendous talent had been underestimated. The tennis experts figured that Tracy still had a way to go before she could knock out the tough, four-time Open winner, Chris Evert-Lloyd.

But in the final match of the tournament, Tracy outsteadied Chris, hammering the ball from the baseline with machine-like precision. When the

match was over, Tracy had won, 6-4, 6-3. When Chris hit the final ball into the net, giving Tracy the victory, Tracy leapt with joy, did a little dance, and rushed up to the net. Chris, once the young champ

who had unseated many top pros, forced a smile and patted her successor on the head.

Tracy was used to pats on the head. She had been beating older players for most of her life. The 16-year-old tennis whiz had been around the game practically from the day she was born.

Tracy was born into a tennis family: her mother and father play, her three brothers play, and her sister plays. Tracy, the youngest Austin, spent the first year of her life in a carriage and playpen outside the fence of a tennis court. The sound of a tennis ball whacking against a racket was an everyday sound to infant Tracy. Vic Braden, tennis pro and family friend, says that when Tracy was eight months old, he was rolling a tennis ball around inside her carriage. "She had a terrible backhand," says Braden.

When Tracy was two years old, she took her first lesson. Her tiny fingers and arms couldn't even hold the racket — until her Dad sawed off the handle and sanded down the grip.

Two-year-old Tracy thought all kids played with tennis rackets. She loved being around the court and taking lessons. And she was always trying to mimic her older brothers and sisters. The Austin family tried to get Tracy to play with dolls. They thought that maybe she felt she *had* to play tennis. But Tracy would look at the dolls, push them aside, and toddle back to hitting tennis balls.

When Tracy was three, her pictures were published in *The Times* of London. When she was four, she was on the cover of *World Tennis*. And it wasn't just because she was cute that she received all that publicity. It was because her tennis game was truly amazing. When Tracy was six, she could beat adults on the tennis court. Tracy's Dad likes to tell about little Tracy walloping some older player on the court and then rushing off to play in the sandbox.

When Tracy was in elementary school, she would

hurry out of class at the end of the day, hop into the back of her mother's station wagon, and change into tennis clothes. Then she would spend hours practicing with girls, boys, and adults.

And she also took a lot of lessons.

When Tracy was 13, her coach, Bob Lansdorp, said, "She can do a little bit of everything. Hit the slice, the drive, even the top spin, although that takes more strength than she's really got. Some time ago she wasn't strong enough to get the ball deep except by floating it. But now she bangs it pretty well. And in another two years she'll be killing top-spin serves. Tracy obviously loves the game. Her temperment is cool, composed; she doesn't get mad. The mark of a champion is to win when you're supposed to. Tracy does. And she doesn't brood over losses, either."

Not that there were many losses. Tracy began to win tournaments almost as soon as she began to enter them. When she was 10, she won the national twelve-and-under championship. When she was 12 and 13, she won the fourteen-and-under title. At 14, she won the eighteen-and-under, and advanced to the quarterfinals of the U.S. Open at Forest Hills.

Tracy was still 14 when she became the youngest player ever invited to compete at Wimbledon. The crowds in London loved her. She was 5'1" tall and dressed in frilly pinafores. The glow in her eyes and the braces on her teeth reminded everyone how young Tracy was.

Tracy ran around Wimbledon in amazement. She stared at the famous players; she gaped at the buildings; she was astounded by the crowds and the vastness of the grounds. "They should put tunnels in this place," she exclaimed at one point. And, "If I eat one more strawberry, I'll throw up."

Two years later, when Tracy walked away with the U.S. Open title, she was three inches taller, and infinitely stronger than the little girl at Wimbledon.

Tracy had turned professional; she earned more than $300,000 in her first year. She had grown accustomed to crowds, big buildings, and even the Wimbledon strawberries. And she had established herself as the number one name in world tennis. No one would ever underestimate Tracy Austin again.